Nerd Life Balance

The Art of Open Sourcing Your Life

Nick Floyd

Nerd Life Balance

The Art of Open Sourcing Your Life

Nick Floyd

To my amazing wife Rebecca and my six excellent kiddos (Caden the programmer, Jonah the hardware blacksmith, Levi the builder, Dylan the adventurer, Ruthie the artist and Avajoy the mad scientist) who were all always so patient with me while I refactored our family for Nerd-life awesome!

And to those at New Relic who not only defined Nerd Life but embody it every day in the amazing software they write.

Contents

The Behavior Parables 89

Foreword

I've always felt that a really good book is a book that you're angry you didn't write. Nick's written that book and you're reading it now. I've struggled with an obsession with productivity while balancing work and family my whole adult life. We're told to work hard now so we can relax and spend time with our loved ones later. Make that money, then achieve those goals, then retire. Unfortunately, it doesn't always work out that way and we often burn out long before we reach the end of the rainbow.

More importantly, we're so busy that we often don't have time to just be. To reflect, and not just to be happy, but to have a moment to breath and even ask the question - am I happy? Are we happy? Is this family doing OK? As nerds we are wired to fix things, to measure things, to analyze things. This is our weakness and our great strength. Nick has put together his experiences and his measurements and his analysis and asked the hard questions for us. He's collected real world experiences from other people like us and synthesized this book as a way to start the right conversations.

With the spirit of Ready Player One and the sensibility of a nerdy Oprah (an Oprah who runs a regular WoW raiding party) Nick's created "Nerd Life Balance." It's a great way for you to start a journey to find balance, your way. Thanks Nick for sharing your experiences and for encouraging us to share ours!"

Scott Hanselman
Parent, Programmer, Professor, Phony
http://hanselman.com[1]

---

[1]http://hanselman.com

Introduction

Over the past several years I've had the privilege of writing code for some seriously amazing companies. Usually, the unspoken mindset was that you were supposed to work until the task was done or that more hours meant more code (good or bad). The thought was by focusing on the tasks and the work, we would inevitably achieve our goals and everyone would be happy. I remember working some really long weeks hitting the work goal, but not feeling very happy. It would be a constant battle to find balance

But here's the challenge for all of those who can relate:

Go for work-life awesome not work-life balance.

This is the idea that you can actually have a job that you are genuinely passionate about and you can live out what you love to do in all aspects of your life.

The great deception is that work and life should be two separate and sterile boxes that need to be measured and weighed by unreachable time-lines and responsibility. This is deceiving because somehow we are convinced that we can't have a job that comes from what we do in life. The sad reality of attempting to serve two separate masters will result in pulling us away from one or the other.

The fact is that our work skills and the rest of our lives are not hot and cold faucets. Instead of becoming frustrated at trying to compartmentalize, we should think about making our lives more congruent. Work skills and talents should not be one-dimensional, but can be thought of as two sides of Velcro that fit together snugly.

With a different mindset, your life can be hitting "work-life awesome." People have attempted to establish balance by completely separating the two, but consider your talents, creativity and passions as a sum rather than a quotient of personal plus work happiness.

Here's the secret: If you find something that you are genuinely excited about and you are fortunate enough to do it as a "job," how awesome would it be to share that passion with your family and friends? It seems logical but we find ourselves returning to the act of trying to peel the two apart again.

I've been writing code for a long time, but it wasn't until more recently, when I joined New Relic, I began to realize that my work is more than part of my life that should be turned off when I left a building. This revelation sprung from New Relic's culture: a place of doers who care tremendously about what they do; a place where every moment is deemed important, not just at work but everywhere; a place where really cool engineering stuff begins at the top and at the bottom; where they'd rather have you over the long run then burn you out early in exchange for some code; a place where family comes first.

Working at New Relic has been challenging and awesome all at the same time, but it has never been work for me. I previously accepted the belief that work always had to be work (which was often frustrating) and that life was the escape from being frustrated at work. But I had it backwards:

> Life is awesome when this thing called "work" becomes another way of expressing the passions in your life.

This book is about finding and expressing what each of us were created to do. You will not find a 12 step approach or some gimmick to be the better you in 10 days. So what is the intent of this book?

The intent of this book is to:

- Help you find the refactoring or "reworking" mindset for your life

- Motivate you toward finding a place that fits your passions
- Help answer that question that has been a constant hum in the back of your mind... "So now what?"
- Start a discussion so that we can all get "better" (not perfect) at this whole work-life thing.

Which means this book is:

- Based on a collection of real world experience from many people
- Intentionally filled with satire and fun to help us all take ourselves a little less seriously
- Filled with Nerd and Geek culture references to illustrate our need for refactoring
- Designed to speak to anyone who is passionate about doing what they love but feel like they can't
- Filled with projects that you can do with your family and friends
- Intended to generate thinking and discussion over what this whole work-life thing is supposed to be.

This book is NOT:

- A self-help book
- Intended to be read but never shared
- Just for "computer" nerds but rather for all nerd-kind

Your time is precious. You're taking time to read this work right now (of which I am grateful) instead of spending that time on other things like playing with the kids, "capturing the flag" in Halo, planting a garden or making your next exhibit for the Maker Faire[2]. Whatever the case, you are here so **THANK YOU**. I have six amazing kids and a beautiful wife, so time and the optimization of getting things done (while having loads of fun) is paramount to me. My hope for you is that the words on the following pages will be valuable to you. Between the over-the-top jokes, histrionic illustrations, smattering of geek/nerd references and all of the stories my desire is that you'll end up finding what I eventually did: **WORK-LIFE AWESOME.**

---

[2]http://makerfaire.com/

A Bit On This Book

Nerd / Geek References: This book is filled to the brim with quotes, perspectives, references and anecdotes from the nerd / geek culture. I'd urge you to "research" any of the references that might seem interesting to you. Of course when I say "research" I mean watch the movie, play the game or interact with the piece of technology mentioned (unless it's a Tardis[3], but if you do would you mind going to the future and letting me know if Half-life 3 ever gets created?).

---

[3]http://en.wikipedia.org/wiki/TARDIS

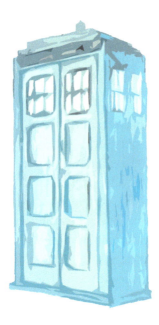

Stories: One of the best ways to illustrate a point is, well through an illustration. You will find illustrations in this book but there are also series of stories that highlight things or provide clarity for some of the more abstract topics covered.

Parables: What's that?! These are simple, short stories that help to teach a lesson. Throughout human history we have used parables whether verbal or written (like in the bible[4]) to help teach thing in creative and clear ways. You're probably wondering why I call these out

---

[4]http://en.wikipedia.org/wiki/Parables_of_Jesus

separately from the **story** content. I do this because when you get to the "parables" section of the book my hope is that you'll find stories that you can not only relate to but learn from as well.

Projects: How can you have a Nerd-life book without nerd-life projects?! You'll discover projects sprinkled throughout this book that are intended to be shared with others. Hopefully these projects will help get you hacking on things with your family and friends, so that you can express your passions and excitement with them in a low friction way. The projects are also in this book so that there is a lower chance that it will end up as part of a monitor stand and act more as a handbook that is used over and over. Please note that all the projects in this book appear in "comic book" form. This serves two purposes:

1. It looks super cool and fits the theme
2. It keeps the projects simple so that they are easy to approach. The idea is to produce motivation and a low friction way to get started.

There is much, much more packed in here but the above are highlights to explain that this is not a typical book. It is more than bits, ink or paper. It is an opportunity to finally go where the dragons are[5]

---

[5] http://en.wikipedia.org/wiki/Here_be_dragons

in your life and see what looking through a Nerd-Life awesome lens is all about.

The Beginning Is The End

In the beginning...

I awoke to the sound of muffled talking, sliding chairs and clicking keyboards. It was Friday morning and I was laying on a sumo chair in one of our pairing rooms. The rooms were no larger than an average meat locker where a butcher might hang the cuts from the previous day. We often used those rooms for storing tables and boxes and sleeping after late night deployments.

My half dead phone was what really woke me up. My wonderfully patient wife asking if she and the kids were going to see me today. Such were many days where I worked. Unpredictable deployments of all types of software late at night easily carried our work into the AM hours. We would catch a few games of Team Fortress while the bits were being rolled out across the servers. It was a good way to pass the time. We laughed between sips of Mountain dew and head-shots.

This is the life we chose for ourselves. Sure we felt pressure from management and product owners to get software out the door but at the end of the day this behavior of slowly killing ourselves with working long hours, eating poorly and stressing out about the confines of a fairly stoic approach Scrum was our choice. The only thing forcing this mindset on us was crumbling expectations and the drive to shoot at the ever-moving target.

I collected all the artifacts that fell out of my pockets during my lengthy nap between the hours of 5:00am and 7:00am and opened the door leading out to the dev pit. It was an open development space with tables, a few orange couches, a thirty foot magnetic scrum wall (we had big plans) and a brick wall. I remember trying to playoff that I was not disoriented from the couple of hours "sleep" and if I could at least make out the lines on the brick wall I'd be OK - ironic isn't it, I'm sure there's a metaphor in there somewhere.

Sometimes I'd slide back to my desk, began sipping

hot Mountain Dew and started to hit the keys again. Other days I'd just go home. Today I decided to head home. I gave a few head nods and courtesy grunts to assure my coworkers that I was in fact not a zombie and headed out the door.

I hopped in my car and began the twenty-four mile drive home. On the clear-minded side of things doing something that could get people hurt like driving while extremely tired is a royally stupid move. Unfortunately, in my mind, I was trained (through reinforcement learning) to do my job this way. I was willing to risk life for something so insignificant because that's what I was conditioned to do.

I didn't know it yet, but this day was going to be different. Today I was going to discover that I had built on something so terrible that it not only almost killed me but I was on my way to leaving something I loved doing - writing software.

Despite my best efforts of windows down, pinching cheeks, slapping my face doing "extreme eyes" with toothpicks, 2 miles from my house I fell asleep and began to head off the into a ditch between the road and train tracks near a parked train. Fortunately, there was another car passing by and he laid on the horn to wake me.

You know those moments when you know you've

drank too much coffee (as if such a thing was actually possible) and you can see your heart pounding out of your chest like a Tom and Jerry cartoon... Yeah, it was a lot like that.

In that moment I decided I was done with software.

It's funny how we often deal in absolutes, as if there is some nagging thirst that can only be quenched by our using the words **always** and **never**. I almost always never struggle with that. I feel that it is the logic boards we have built into us; forcing absolution out of us just as easily as pressing keys on our keyboards to create 1's and 0's.

We are more than that. More than what we do at work or at home. Have you ever had a burning thought that you could never shake; like trying to put down a can of Pringles but quickly returning to it uttering the "just one more" catch phrase of addiction?

When I said I was going to put down software that day it was a claim made in vain. I couldn't do it. The fact was that writing code made me smile, it was part of my inner nerd and it wasn't going away. I couldn't put down the software developer can of Pringles and I knew it, so I just decided that there was a better way to eat this thing called work-life balance.

If I was going to be the husband, the dad, the developer and the person I needed to be I was going to have to start living in a new balance - a Nerd Life Balance.

I know what you're thinking, "wow, another smattering of words that is going to tell me how to be a better me!" or "a book that will help me understand balance better." No, I'm here to tell you that is not at all what this is about. It's about making a difference and making an impact.

I've done this software developer thing for about twenty years now. In that time I have been part of a few startups, a few really large companies and even started up a few companies of my own. Eighteen of those twenty years I have slept under desks, in closets, worked without seeing my family for some time, destroyed my health and my family. I wasn't alone in my destruction and even worse, I was often the one encouraging those behaviors.

Many of my fellow workers, the people I coded with and managed did the same. We all seemed to have one goal, ship software and destroy ourselves in the process. It was as if we were disposable copper top batteries, plugged into the matrix waiting to run out of useful energy. Only until recently (the last few years) do I feel like I have finally been doing this Nerd-life thing "right" and living life with genuine enthusiasm first and finding "balance" in that.

In an article posted by Emma Jacobs of the Financial

Times was quoted saying:

> "Most efforts fail if we aim for work-life balance as it's superficial unless you change how work is done."

I love that. It states one simple and clear point of view... what we've been doing all these years, trading hours of our lives for sheets of paper or pixels on the screen; it's not working.

Throughout my entire career there were only a few times that I was told that I need to stay late and get things done; not that there wasn't "implied" pressure or expectations. There was a lot of that. The point is that at any time I could have made a choice, a choice to say "No" or I could have accepted the obvious fact that the work will be there tomorrow. So why didn't I?

I love being a developer. I love that I can create something that will genuinely delight someone else. I love failing when I try something new and working to get better at it. I love that the work I do gives me challenging problems to solve. Most of all I love solving those problems and "winning." I call this the "**Skinner effect**" and I believe that is why many of us struggle with spending long hours at this physical place called work.

My idea of the "Skinner effect" comes from the research B.F. Skinner did using his operant conditioning chamber (The "Skinner Box" - which, incidentally B.F. Skinner did not like his device being called a Skinner Box). The idea is simple, we are rewarded for "winning" and punished for "loosing." Everything we do as developers tends to lead to behavioral reinforcement in some way, shape or form.

Game theory calls this reinforcement learning. It simply states that, "more successful behaviors tend to be held more tenaciously and will occur more frequently."

Every time we build our software or run our tests we get feedback. We are constantly being rewarded in small increments for getting it right or scolded by our test runners for getting it wrong. I won't get into all of the research done on our brains, dopamine and the anticipation of success but I do want to point out that this is both a psychological and physiological thing.

Just observe developers that are near a solution in the software they have written - you'll see them unable to leave the keyboard, as if they have been physically connected to it. Basic needs such as food and the bathroom breaks quickly become optional when we are on the edge of solving something.

Second only to this, in my opinion, is the idea that we are really poor estimators of time and effort. Ask any developer have they ever lost track of time when working on a hard problem? Developers can be considered the "eternal external optimists" - while on the inside we are burning with uncertainty and desire to solve the seemingly unsolvable problem.

As far as estimating, ask the same developers to estimate a problem that has never been solved and you'll get a ton of sheepish grins around the table. Our minds spin on the incalculable scenarios we might run into while solving the problem and we even begin to thread out solutions to the unknown. Developers are amazing creatures, we can be both confident and completely uncertain about a problem and how to solve it simultaneously.

It's like playing one of the seemingly millions of mobile games. We find ourselves captivated by the brilliant yet simple design. It feels familiar somehow, like the smell of Halloween. We are mystified by the "amazing" game play and the perceived story. Here's the rub: it is just an excellent deception. Once you peel back the facade of crushable candy or sparkly gems sliding majestically across the screen you see something that is absolutely captivating to any psychologist. You see a Skinner box. A box whose walls are constructed of in-app purchases, amazing marketing and gamification. The reality is that there are some seriously smart people who are paid to come up with ways to keep you in the game. Next time you are "playing" (or more appropriately, being owned by) one of those games and it rattles off "AMAZING!" or prompts you with a "free" spin, consider this: **who is playing who?**

I know this sounds a bit harsh but we are addressing one of the Nerd world's greatest deceptions: the idea that we are in control because we have the keyboard. There are innumerable variables to the work-life equation which often cause the final calculation to be irrational. So then how does one stop the madness? How do you know if there is even any madness to begin with? We are, after all, problem solvers, over achievers and hard workers. We are nerds and this prospect of defeat will not drag us down it will only make us stronger!

An author from wikipedia defines Nerd as:

> Nerd[6] is a descriptive term, often used pejoratively, indicating that a person is overly intellectual, obsessive, or socially impaired. They may spend inordinate amounts of time on unpopular, obscure, or non-mainstream activities, which are generally either highly technical or relating to topics of fiction or fantasy, to the exclusion of more mainstream activities.[1][2][3] Additionally, many nerds are described as being shy, quirky, and unattractive,[4] and may have difficulty participating in, or even following, sports. Though originally derogatory, "Nerd" is a stereotypical term, but as with other pejoratives, it has been reclaimed and redefined by some as a term of pride and group identity.

After reading that I'm sure some might think, "Wow,

---

[6] http://en.m.wikipedia.org/wiki/Nerd

nope not me - I am not a nerd!" To which I will reply, "Reread the last part of that definition."

"Though originally derogatory, "Nerd" is a stereotypical term, but as with other pejoratives, it has been reclaimed and redefined by some as a term of pride and group identity."

Year	Spelling	Published	Context
1950	Nerd	If I Ran The Zoo	A small humanoid creature looking comically angry, like a thin, cross Chester A. Arthur.
1951	Nerd	Newsweek	Someone who once would be called a drip or a square (Detroit slang: extreme form of *scurve*

Year	Spelling	Published	Context
1952	Nerd	St. Joseph, Michigan Herald-Press	Synonym for *scurve*, opposite of George. Also a drip.
1957	Nerd	Glasgow, Scotland Sunday Mail	"ABC for SQUARES": "Nerda square, any explanation needed?"
1961	Millard Fillmore Nerd	Swarthmore College Hamburg Show	Name of a self-confessed square, who has not broken a single rule
1965	Nurd	RPI Bachelor	Used to refer to 61 students
1970	Nurd [sic]	Current Slang	Someone with objectionable habits or traits.... An uninteresting person, a 'dud.'

Year	Spelling	Published	Context
1980	Nerd or Nurd	Slang	An over-studious person, esp a computer devotee
2000s	Nerd	Slang	Began being transposed with the term geek though the two terms have distinct meanings
2015	Nerd	Nerd Life Balance	An individual who is genuinely passionate about something and who wants to share it with everyone

Table derived from reference.com[7]

It is my opinion that this last section is really the only true meaning of what a nerd today is. The word no

---

[7] http://dictionary.reference.com/browse/nerd

longer follows the stereotype of its origin from the 1950's Dr. Seuss book, If I ran the Zoo[8].

Let me see if I can give some perspective. Say, for instance, you love computers. Everything about them excites you; if there is a new processor that hit the market you're already working up when you're going to buy one (at least) and how you might over clock it because you love getting the most out of the experience of tweaking. You are constantly talking about it with anyone who will listen and challenge your ideas. Additionally you feel compelled to share this passion with anyone who might want to learn. One might say that you are indeed a "computer nerd."

Now let's say you were the type of person who loves gardening. (Word of caution: given that I know absolutely nothing about plants other than: 1. some smell and look nice and 2. some you can eat. Hopefully this example will help to "grow" the thought.)

Everything about plants excites you; if there is a new bulb ready for planting that you see at the local nursery you've already worked up how many you need to make you home garden experience perfect. You are constantly talking about it with anyone who will listen and challenge your ideas. Additionally you feel compelled to share this passion with anyone who

---

[8]http://en.wikipedia.org/wiki/If_I_Ran_the_Zoo

might want to learn. One might say that you are indeed a "Garden nerd."

So what's the difference other than personal hygiene and number of cans of energy drinks consumed (sorry, I couldn't help raising the sarcastic stereotype flag - believe it or not gardeners probably do have good hygiene)? Nothing really. There is one key aspect to this thinking: if you are passionate about something and you're compelled to share it, then you just might be a nerd and if you are... read on.

The Problem

So here's the part where I act like I have seen so much over the past several years and I have been able to come up with a logical conclusion to why humanity is, in general, addicted to work and why we have somehow reinvented success to be a hilltop without friends, family and moral absolutes.

While I hate to disappoint and tell you up front that there is not just one singular issue or broken behavior that leads to work leaching from life or vice versa I have messed it up long enough to be able run down many of the patterns that tend to destroy the balance. There is one underlying hum that I'd like I suggest could be the main glitch in the Matrix. I'm not so sure that this vibration in the ship's hull is the cause of all of the breaking points but I do think it's a good place to begin.

Trying to define the behaviors that tend to drive us to distraction is much like working on a bug in your code and realizing you've just awoken the never-ending hurt locker swarm. You know that just by simple logic there is an end to the ball of yarn you're unraveling but eventually it becomes a journey of faith, fire and fury.

This leads us to the fundamental flaw of perceived perfection. Do you remember when you were a kid; a time where you were limited by bed times and cash flow? Ignorance is bliss, is it not - to paraphrase the eager to leave the "real life" Cypher. As kids we don't "know better" and we think anything is possible. I draw heavily from my kids unbounded passions when we are working on projects. They have that super power that rips right through the bureaucracy of adulthood and says "I've got a better idea."

It's like blowing into your Nintendo cartridges (you know you did it) knowing that they might work again and "power gloving" right through a problem that had no real answer. We didn't know so we didn't have anything to fear like failure or pretense.

What would happen if we all lived in a world where we replaced our "you can't" with "let's try." Our "I have an idea" with "git init, git commit and git push?" I'm not talking about the self-help crap of positive thinking; I'm drawing on genuine faith that blowing in the cartridges just might work.

Consider Thomas Edison when he said, "Many of life's failures are people who did not realize how close they were to success when they gave up." The problem with the perfection syndrome is that if we are always beginning or pursuing perfect then how will we know we've arrived?

The image of the ideal rarely ever matches reality. This sticks us with a pile of garbage that is effectively ineffective. The pursuit of the perfect has destroyed empires, countries, relationships and really great soft drinks (Crystal Pepsi, need I say more?).

So how do you win at a job that never seems done, where the endgame is an illusion? We seem to be at an unimaginable impasse, an unfortunate fork in the tale. I believe there is an answer and that we can solve for "x" but we'll get to that later, let's finish defining the problem.

So atop perfection sits the unquenchable human trigger to win, beat the man, pull of the heist, provide shock and awe to our users and to be recognized and rewarded for it.

Now before we go too far I want to make sure that I am clear about the "recognized and rewarded" piece of this puzzle. I believe that much of the makers, developers and creators who are genuinely excited about what they do are not narcissistic. They talk about what they do because they want everyone else to be just as excited as they are about the "thing" and that's the reward and recognition.

So far so good, doing really great and exciting things, check. Winning at those things, check. So where's the problem?

It's success.

Over the years "success" has presented itself in many ways. From building things during the industrial revolution, idealized peace in the 60's or money and cars (insert your favorite 80's or 90's rap cassette tape if you've forgotten capitalism at its peak).

The idea is not that "success" is bad; that's like when people misquote the bible and say, "money is the root of all evil." No, no it's not. My large bills sporting Washington have never become a couple of kids that were up to no good, who started making trouble in my neighborhood.

The problem is in how success is portrayed and defined. If you were able to escape thoughts of the "Fresh Prince of Bel-Air"[9] a few sentences back then you, my friend, have massive mental fortitude or you've never heard of the pauper made prince TV extravaganza.

The story was simple, a kid growing up in a "rough" part of town gets into some trouble and his mom sends him to live with his "auntie" and "uncle" in BelAir. When he gets there he is enthralled by the glamor of it all but he quickly finds that it's not all "perfect."

Expectations + circumstantially defined success = null

*   *   *

Here's a thought, what if success or winning with this whole work and life thing **did not** mean the following:

---

[9]http://en.wikipedia.org/wiki/The_Fresh_Prince_of_Bel-Air

What if there was a fourth option? An option where instead of treating work and life like sand paper we treated it more like Velcro?

We burn so many cycles trying to keep our heads and our schedules in check so that we can give each compartment what it's due. How frustrating! Talk about the Rube Goldberg[10] path of life - a never-ending complex set of paths and steps to do something so seemingly simple - live life to the full!

Try taking a stab at the following exercise. Given that I hate it when speakers or writers ask me to participate I'll give you the answer: the math does not work and time is not on your side.

*　　*　　*

For those of you who really want to know, let's do the following: to the best of your ability fill in the sections below with a guess of how much time you spend in a week on each thing. Keep in mind, the sum of all time recorded cannot exceed 168 hours (one week).

Take this as an opportunity to laugh at the ridiculous nature of our schedules and possibly go share it with friends and family to see how they rank. Hopefully together we can all gain something from openly thinking about these things in new ways and encourage each other with shared solutions and ideas.

---

[10]http://en.wikipedia.org/wiki/Rube_Goldberg_machine

Act	Time spent
Average time spent sleeping	__ hr(s)
Average time spent eating	__ hr(s)
Average time spent on the potty	__ hr(s)
Average time spent getting dressed / showering	__ hr(s)
Average time spent with family	__ hr(s)
Average time spent with friends	__ hr(s)
Average time spent working	__ hr(s)
Average time spent driving	__ hr(s)
Average time spent hacking / making / creating	__ hr(s)
Average time spent playing video games	__ hr(s)
Average time spent staring at the wall	__ hr(s)
Average time spent on [_____]	__ hr(s)
Average time spent on [_____]	__ hr(s)
Average time spent on [_____]	__ hr(s)
TOTAL	___ hr(s)

TOTAL SHOULD BE < 168 (unless you are The Doctor and have a Tardis[11]).

---

[11]http://en.wikipedia.org/wiki/TARDIS

The Great Deception

If you took the little "test" from the previous chapter you might be feeling a bit deflated or perhaps overwhelmed. Hopefully it helped you consider new ways to re-factor your life. You might also be feeling that there's been a grand lie that has been passed around since humanity began counting hours. The following **lie** is deceptively simple yet really, really effective at helping us defeat ourselves.

> "There are 168 hours in every week and if I am going to use it wisely I must compartmentalize."

Ok, so perhaps that's not a completely "true" lie. Let

me try that again...

> "There are 168 'usable' hours in every
> week and if I am going to use it wisely
> I must compartmentalize."

The fact is that we have black holes and dynamos eating and generating the little time we have here on this earth. Somethings we do absorb the mass of time we have, while other things we do can sometimes feel like they help generate "new" time.

In 1979 there was a science fiction film named "The Black Hole[12]." I had the book and record that went with the movie which I played at least few thousand times. The robot on the U.S.S Palomino named V.I.N.C.E.N.T remarked,

> "A black hole, the deadliest force in the
> universe, nothing can escape it!"

That is an amazingly accurate description concerning all the time we don't seem to have, how that time passes so quickly or how easily it is wasted. There are always gaps in time, leaky moment faucets that cause the time we have to simply disappear. There

---

[12]http://en.wikipedia.org/wiki/The_Black_Hole

are ways to deal with the theoretical gravity of your minute draining anomaly, but first you have to accept that this framework called TIME is a bit of a farce. Not because it is not scientific or that it has not been proven as a metric that can be measured and used - no, the problem with time has nothing to do with time at all. Our age-old struggle with time has all to do with us and our effective utilization of a limited resource that has no perceptible limit outside of death.

It is as though we treat time more like Tribbles[13] and less like a scarce resource. We measure it loosely against the beginning of time and see no reason to be concerned that as an individual consumer we can only eat so much.

It's a lot like eating Pringles; for some reason you can't stop consuming the salty round tricksters but then suddenly the can is empty and your eyes are open to the fact that each of the 300 unstoppable pops tasted less like a potato chip and more like regret. So you reach for your Mountain Dew friend and drown your snacking sorrows. Perhaps we can bail on the sorrow and snack on our time using a healthier treat. I know what you're thinking, "I love my 'B' movies and my sixteen hour stretches of Bioshock Infinite[14]

---

[13]http://en.wikipedia.org/wiki/Tribble
[14]http://en.wikipedia.org/wiki/BioShock_Infinite

and League of Legends[15] tourneys'." While I would agree that those things are a possible staple of a type of Nerd's life, I feel like I must share a truth with you:

"The Nerd cannot live on 'game' alone."

"Heresy!" you say?

Recently I was chatting with a software developer friend of mine. We were discussing if participating in a hackathon would be something that was worth doing. I asked her if it was a technology that was interesting and so on and from there we continued talking about the pros and cons of participating. We ended the conversation with this simple, yet powerful dialog:

> "her: I'm interested in all of it [game development] and I think it would be fun to try."

> "me: here's the deal... worst case if you participate you don't finish the game but you would've at least learned something"

---

[15]http://en.wikipedia.org/wiki/League_of_Legends

"her: true."

"me: we're not guaranteed tomorrow, why put off to tomorrow what you could do today?"

It sounds cliche, I know, but it's a very applicable perspective. Putting off doing something often feels easier than doing it. I have always wondered what would happen if we were ever to place a constraint on ourselves that a certain percentage of the meetings we were in had to be a type of working meeting. A meeting where things actually happened instead of a bunch of people just talking about the things that needed to be done. Don't get me wrong meetings have their function, but what if we could simply begin working on the things that needed to be done.

I struggle with this idea of getting rid of ideas and just starting a project when it's conceived. I talk myself into and out of some projects that have potential.

In the case above, as we were talking I was downloading the SDK (Software Development Kit) and had created a new repository for the game; I left our conversation motivated, inspired even.

Will it become something? I don't know.

Will I regret trying to create something new? Probably not.

Will I learn something that I might be able to share with others? Definitely.

Motivation is a powerful force that can give ideas the momentum needed to become projects. Motivation presses the keys on our keyboards when we don't want to; it pushes us a bit harder when we are questioning sharing a new idea with our friends or family. It's the warp core[16] to the nacelles of our lives; the redstone[17] to our building blocks.

The problem with motivation is that it can be a snare just as much as it can be freeing. Most of the time you'll find developers working pretty hard on the things they do. If you ask them why do they work so passionately a common response might be:

> "Because I want to build something that will delight people and that I can be proud of."

We have to be careful of this type of motivational compulsion because if we base our self-worth in the

---

[16]http://en.wikipedia.org/wiki/Warp_drive
[17]http://minecraft.gamepedia.com/Redstone

depths of the things we create and how people respond to those things we could fall into Corporate Stockholm Syndrome[18]. Not to mention people are emotional and fickle; humans emotionally swing like pendulums that can either delight you with praise or beat you down with disappointment.

If we frequently find ourselves in situations where we are "expected" to stay late and do "whatever it takes" to get the job done we might be suffering from this trap. This type of emotional trauma can cause some serious damage. If I had to put it into "gamer" terms it would be like facing Gordon Freeman's crowbar[19]. There will be a lot of swings but the one on the receiving end of the bar will always go down.

---

[18]http://en.wikipedia.org/wiki/Stockholm_syndrome
[19]http://en.wikipedia.org/wiki/Gordon_Freeman

Inspiration and motivation can completely backfire on us. We can go to a great talk at a conference or talk to someone who has infectious energy, like a "energy drink" with legs, but on the other side of that we leave feeling like we can do anything without thinking about why we'd even want to do what we just got persuaded to do.

I think some of the greatest lies we could tell ourselves is that we'll do x later or that saying "yes" to everything is the best way to level up. It seems that these two things are contradictions of one another but instead of falling on the far extremes of each, perhaps there is a way to balance the "yes" and "no" moments in our lives. Use the following checklist to see if you might have more black holes than dynamos in your life:

Phrase	Times said
I'll do that next week...	x
I don't have time...	x
I'll do x later...	x
In just a minute...	x
There is always time for x...	x
Hey let's catch up later...	x
We should meet for x sometime...	x
I need to do x...	x
Other	x

I pretty much fail this test every time I take it. Just recently I discovered something really important. So important that it has completely changed the way I communicate and the way I think. It is something I am still practicing and still getting wrong. Here's what I discovered:

"No is a complete sentence."

Saying no to things I simply cannot do is hard. The fact is there are just some things that we simply cannot do. Either they just do not fit our passion or they do not align with our priorities; whatever the case, a simple "No" can go a really long way. When we justify our actions it can come across to most people like Hollywood trying to convince the technically savvy to accept their latest Hacker disaster-piece. It sounds and feels ridiculous.

Justification is simply another way to defer dealing with something else. The fact is that time is finite and our consumption of that construct is paramount. How we consume it is critical. It's like running around in Half-Life[20] and using up all the health and suit chargers before trying to down the boss - the chargers will be used up and you'll have nothing left for the second wave.

Do you believe we have a tendency to lie to ourselves? I do. If we could more purposely use what we have, it would keep us from insanity driven behaviors like compartmentalization and time paralysis.

When we take chunks of things and stick them in compartments the space between those compartments is lost. Sometimes when I have stared at broken bit of code or problem for a while I need a new perspective. Often my kids are that perspective. Children show this amazing ability to see past all the cruft we as "seasoned" humans tend to put on our lives. Our mindset of "you cannot" or "you should not" become their "why not."

I was working on an application that cached some pages. Naturally, the challenge I was facing was around

---

[20]http://en.wikipedia.org/wiki/Half-Life_%28video_game%29

cache invalidation[21]. I had been banging my head on this issue off and on for about a month until one day I came home and my seven-year old asked me what was on my mind. I told him what the problem was (we do that sort of thing in my household - sharing hard problems for perspective). He then replied with a statement that shattered my little developer world:

> "If it's causing you so many problems why don't you just stop using it?"

In an instant my son single-handedly solved one of the hardest problems in computer science[22]. With his suggestion in mind I removed the code and all was well.

You see, the great deception isn't something sneaky someone else does to us, rather, it's something we convince ourselves of. Who you are at work and at home really should be the same person because you **are** the same person. We are free to bring our nerd home and share it with our family and friends; we owe it to them! So ask yourself, "Do you think you are behaving like the individual you are and want to be?"

---

[21]http://en.wikipedia.org/wiki/Cache_invalidation
[22]http://martinfowler.com/bliki/TwoHardThings.html

The 3D Expectation

There has not been one time that I have started a project and didn't already have a picture of what it would be or do. It was a lot like that with me and my kids early on before I got the whole Nerd-Life thing. I had this picture that they would be "perfect" in every way, always obey, always listen to the amazing wisdom that I was going to impart on them and of course, be interested in everything I was interested in.

Fortunately it didn't turn out that way. Where's the adventure in a predictable everything; especially when it comes to the amazing nature of kids? There is none. Zip! Zilch! /dev/null[23]! Nil! Null!

One of the most exciting aspects of our lives is the unknown. You know, where the dragons are. A long

---

[23]http://en.wikipedia.org/wiki/Null_device

time ago when a cartographer charted the known land they would draw out these marvelous maps with fantastic precision and on most of the maps there would be uncharted territories. Often times the artist would put the words "here be the dragons." This was meant to inform or alert the person using the map that the things in this area could be dangerous and are unknown. Much like the fog of war in Warcraft[24], Star-Craft[25] and most dungeon crawlers today; it means either wondrous discovery or instant death!

The fear or acceptance of the unknown is powerful. It will either motivate you or tear you apart.

My daughter, three years old at the time, approached me and asked if she could "maker" something - she called it that because when we don't know what project to do we often say "be a 'maker' first and let the project worry about itself." She knew her four brothers loved building and breaking stuff, it was only a matter of time before she would be sitting at my desk sorting through bread boards and solder, wanting to make something.

Let me set the stage a bit before I continue. All of the kids in my house learn to solder, use tools and work with software starting at a really early age. This tradition of cutting one's "maker" teeth early came about when I sat down at my desk one day and there was a stack of toys sitting on my desk. Various electronics, talking stuffed animals and even a laptop (not even sure where that came from) littered my maker shrine. In all honesty my desk usually looks like a Radio Shack threw up on it but I knew things had finally gone too far.

"This is madness!" I shouted.

My ever so wise and beautiful wife knew what I was belting out about.

"Nope it's part of who you are to the kiddos. They know you fix stuff."

At this point I was dumb founded, flattered and of course humbled. The thought that my kids count on me passed through my head; so why did I feel like I was doing them a disservice?

"Well sure, that's true but I don't want to raise a bunch of 'users'. I mean not like a TRON user because they were cool programmers and all. You know the kind that just use but don't create."

My wife smirked at my irresistible nerd charm and I knew exactly where she was about to take this conversation.

"Yup, sounds like you need to teach them to fish."

She was of course referring to "Give a person a fish and feed them for a day, teach them to fish and feed them for a life time." and she was right. My expectation was that they would simply inherit the mad hacking skills from me and we would have a house full of brilliant minds running around doing science. Additionally, I had this ache in the back of my head that things would break and it would take "longer" to get things done. This was, of course, my expectation trying to override who I knew I needed to be.

Just then my four-year old came around the corner with another toy in tow as if to say "hey dad here's an opportunity to apply what you just learned." I took him by the hand and said, "Kiddo, today you're going to solder this back together." The kids now "repair" their own toys. Does it always work? Not a chance! Does it end up breaking more things? Sometimes. Are my kids makers? You'd better believe it!

We can either continue to assume our friends and family have nothing to learn from us and continue to be the person they call to fix their stuff, or we can teach them to fish.

Now back to my little girl. She had seen her brothers wield the amazing smoking utensil, otherwise known as the soldering iron, and she did not want to have anything to do with it. She had firmly established an expectation that she would get hurt by it and rooted an assumption in her amazing mind that she would not like to use it at all.

I started by soldering something with her in my lap, then moved to her holding the rosin core and finally to me holding her hand while she soldered with me. After a bit she warmed up to the idea of using it. Now she wants to do all the soldering for her brother's projects.

TIP: For parents who want to introduce your kids to soldering, hunt down a simple soldering project like one listed in this book or get a fun kit. Then turn the temperature up on your gun, 400 or 450 degrees Fahrenheit should do it. This will cause it to smoke a bit while you work together on a project. It will probably end up giving you more messy connections but singeing the solder will make little smoke plumes that seem almost magical. (**NOTE:** make sure not to breathe in the fumes and have a really well ventilated area.) **ALWAYS** make sure you are taking the proper precautions - kids are absolutely one of the most unpredictable creatures on the planet; do your best to have an environment that is both safe and productive to learning.

Before I realized how good setting appropriate expectations could be I was a train wreak when my kids
wanted to help me with a build. The constant barrage
of "be careful of this" and "don't hold it like that"
really stole a potentially wonderful experience from
me and my kids.

In 1991 Appogee Software released Duke Nukem[26].
Mixed with its questionable overtones and quipping
protagonist many people fell in love with the game. A
few years later the studio announced that they were
working on the most technically amazing version of
this game which eventually became known as Duke
Nukem Forever[27]. This game was in "development" for
fifteen years (from 1996 to 2011) across four different
game studios.

Buzz built around the studio's project for years. There
was speculation after speculation and each more ridiculous than the last. The studio struggled with putting
teeth into the project. They changed the underlying
architecture and game engine on more than one occasion and scope creep swallowed any efforts to build

[26]http://en.wikipedia.org/wiki/Duke_Nukem_%28video_game%29
[27]http://en.wikipedia.org/wiki/Development_of_Duke_Nukem_Forever

something stable. It seemed like problem after problem and change after change made the game one of the most ironically titled in computer gaming history.

What happened? Expectation overrode reality. The leaders there had an ever-changing picture of what they thought the game should be. I am sure there were other factors but the sentiment of failing to meet a vision will always be an attribute overcasting the game's legacy. Later on another studio picked up the project and delivered it, but some argued that the studio knew that even if they delivered something they would really never be able to deliver on the legendary myth woven by expectation.

Kingdoms rise and fall because of expectations and assumptions. Billions of dollars change hands in the stock market from a set of pre-constructed expectations. Historically, we as a human race have not really ever been very good at predicting the future. Time and time again we try to take on the role of the X-Man Bishop[28] and jump through time in designing software, planning for life, making and even in simple conversations with each other - making lousy attempts at trying to finish someone else's thought with partial information and crummy assumptions.

We could print anything!

---

[28]https://en.wikipedia.org/wiki/Bishop_(comics)

Ah 3D printing. Now that 3D printers are getting to be affordable they have begun find their ways into both the "technical" and non-technical households. Kickstarter is filled with manufacturers trying their hand at the 3D printer consumer market. Avoiding the plethora of Kickstarter clones we got a PrintrBot Simple Metal kit[29]. When we got the kit my kids, true to form, responded with "cool what are we going to make now?!" After stating that it was a 3D printer they seemed unimpressed so we jaunted over to YouTube and watched a few time laps videos of 3D prints. They still seemed a bit unclear on what it was all about.

Fortunately, I had five enthusiastic kids ready to put together the puzzle of a thousand pieces. To set a picture upfront, yes we lost some pieces (that was "expected") but they were easy to replace and well worth the experience of working on a project together.

Once we finished constructing the 3-axis beast we all became intrigued. Admittedly I didn't even know what to expect. One of the first things you do after building the printer is calibrate it using a little square model. After sorting through a walk through on getting setup the smell of PLA filament began to fill the room (it smelled a little like waffles) as the extruder started to heat up. Then it began. The printer was

---

[29]http://en.wikipedia.org/wiki/Printrbot

shifting quickly on all 3-axis' and it was nothing short of mesmerizing!

We were all locked in and we stood in silence as we watched it print a 3-dimensional square. I saw each of my children begin to understand what was unfolding before their eyes. "We could print anything!" was the catalyst for the most interesting conversation about project ideas that we have ever had as a family. They got it. They understood that the imagination is limitless without considering implementation. With tools that help blur the line between thought and reality the little scientists realized that combination could literally change the world. We jumped from ideas of printing toys to printing hearts for humans. They got it and all it took was a 3-dimentional square printed with filament made from corn.

Stop for a minute and realize that you and I live in THAT world, right here, right now. A world where we can make the choice to do amazing things and be so much more than "users." We can create!

A bit on 3D Printing

3D printing is a process by which a 3D model is provided to a machine and a physical 3-dimensional object is created. Conceptually it is much like 2D printing (paper and ink) except that it uses a filament instead of ink and physical space instead of paper.

There are a few different approaches to 3D printing; a couple of the most common ones are additive and subtractive.

Additive 3D printing uses a 3D model generated by software which is then "sliced" by some other software which results in a file containing both the sliced 3D object and some meta data. This file is then given to the printer which uses a 3-axis plane to print layers, additively, until the whole model is rendered in physical space. Additive printing can use many types of filaments such as PLA[30] (polylactic acid), ABS[31] (Acrylonitrile Butadiene Styrene), concrete, liquid resin and even things like chocolate or cheese. The hardware for this type of printing is generally inexpensive (excluding industrial printers) and the filament is low-cost as well. Additive often uses a process called extrusion where layer by layer material is extruded from a source and the model is built. Conceptually speaking it is simple but when you observe it first-hand it is mind-blowing!

Equally as "mind-blowing" subtractive 3D printing. This is the process by which material is stripped away or subtracted from a source material to create the 3-dimensional model in physical space. This process can use things like high pressure water systems and lasers

---

[30]http://reprap.org/wiki/PLA
[31]http://reprap.org/wiki/ABS

to remove the material from the source.

> TIP: If you are using a filament based printer and do not have a heated bed you will probably want to avoid using an ABS filament and just stick with PLA. ABS typically is a bit more flexible than its PLA counterpart which makes it a bit more difficult for the model to stay in place due to vibrations, movement of the extruder and connected material on the printer bed. Also, without a "heated" plate for your printer you might want to try the combination of blue painter's tape on the bed, sanding the taped surface and then lightly cleaning the taped and sanded surface by using alcohol (70% ISO). Oils from your skin prevent the filament from sticking to the surface which will quickly end up in filament spaghetti instead of your intended model.

Since our first step into 3D printing we have had many failed prints and have had to realign our expectations on this whole 3D movement. It's hard not to picture this wonderful world where you're the captain on the bridge saying "Tea, Earl gray, Hot" to a replicator after printing a model you created. While we are not at a point where we can manipulate energy into tea I cannot escape the feeling that one day we will see something like a Star Trek replicator as Gene Roddenberry envisioned. Though, I probably shouldn't set my expectations too high.

What are some of the road blocking expectations that are stopping you from taking your 2D idea and making it a 3D reality?

The Paradox

I HAVE NO IDEA HOW I GOT HERE.

It was a cold and rainy September day and I was riding down the Springwater corridor in Portland, Oregon. Nodding mindlessly to the opposing riders or throwing a bell ring at those I was sharing the trail with.

I was trapped by a thought; captivated by a problem. It was something I was carrying away from my desk at work. This made it difficult to focus on much of anything else. Given that I had gone down both the road of thought and the Springwater many times before I felt I could handle the multitasking.

The funny thing about pride through familiarity: you end up missing out on so many beautiful things around you and you usually end up with a tail between your legs because your perceived success ends in actual disaster. This time was no different.

I hit a railroad track that was running at a rough forty-five degrees to the road I was on. The rail groove was just wide enough for my tire to get caught in the crossing causing me to be thrown like a rag doll that you might see in one of those seriously fun physics games. I was so completely enthralled by my problem solving that I didn't even notice I had been thrown off until I hit the ground. I thought to myself, "I have no idea how I got here."

For me this was a brutal truth over the first twenty or so years of my career. It started out as an "I got this" moment and usually ended up with me stressed out over a project or two and me sleeping under my desk or on top of a table. Maybe you can relate. Maybe you've had moments where you've looked up and wondered "how did I get myself into this situation?" Like boiling a frog, this "work and then life mentality" will enviably cook you and us.

I laid there on the ground. Wet, cold with a searing pain in my knee. I just laid there in frustration over my spectacular flight but even more displeased that I had completely forgotten all that I had processed over the course of the eight mile ride from the office to the ground where I was laying. I rolled over on my back, winced and looked into the gray nether (more commonly known as Portland sunshine).

A car passed me and honked as to say to me "watch out for that track; haven't you ever ridden a bike before!" I picked myself up with my extra slice of humble pie and a lot of respect for train tracks. I limped home over the next five miles with plenty of time to consider what had happened.

At that moment I was doing two things I loved: biking and solving a really hard software problem. Here's the part where you might expect me to launch into the "multitasking is a myth" monologue. I'll save you from the droning and just put it this way: some call it multitasking, some call it multi-threading; I like to think of it as Multi-distracting.

Multi-distracting, simply put, is attempting to focus on more than one thing that you are really passionate about. Linda Stone[32] coined a term that closely represents the phenomenon of soaking in bits and pieces of

---

[32]http://en.wikipedia.org/wiki/Linda_Stone

the world around us as continual partial attention[33]. It's the idea of collecting a lot of data but never going deep with any of it.

It's the Lawnmower Man effect[34]. Achieve "genius" through sampling everything and experiencing nothing. We are all familiar with this idea; in biblical terms it is called "trying to serve two masters." It would be like trying to learn Kung fu while learning Jiu Jitsu at the same time and doing it without the luxury of the Matrix! One does not simply live two lives and download all the things Neo.

It's that ache in the back of your head when you put on the Lawnmower Man VR headset and just start munching through the motions and the billions of bits flying toward you. So instead of doing one thing really well you do two or more things at half pace.

So then how do you live a passionate life while doing the things you love with those you love? How do you live like you are going to fall of your bike without actually falling off?

You hack time using tools like realistic expectations and planning.

I love a really good "weekend hack." One where you

---

[33]http://en.wikipedia.org/wiki/Continuous_partial_attention
[34]http://en.wikipedia.org/wiki/The_Lawnmower_Man_%28film%29

simply cannot get the idea out of your head and you've got to bend some metal, solder some connections or throw some bits just to breathe. Some of the best sessions that I have had around these ideas were with good friends.

A few years ago I connected with a couple of software developers and we decided that we were going to do fifty-two projects in a year, one each weekend. The goal was simple: do a seriously fun hack, learn something and share it with others. We did all of those things but after a while it began to get to be too much. I had a new baby on the way and we were all working at a place where we were not upholding the best work-life balances. It was good but it was time to end it. I still have weekend hacks. Six kids later and I'm either working with those amazing kids or taking some alone time and get something knocked out.

Before moving on, you'll notice I mentioned getting some "alone time" which implies doing a project by yourself. My default on almost all the projects I do will be to BAF (see chapter seven) but there are times when Mr. Furious[35] rides in a wolf pack of one. Some projects call for a Deus Ex[36] approach of taking on the futuristic terror of undone projects alone and those can be equally as amazing, just make sure to share

---

[35] http://en.wikipedia.org/wiki/Mystery_Men
[36] http://en.wikipedia.org/wiki/Deus_Ex

the results with others when you're done!

So what changed between then and now? The difference now is that the projects are planned and on purpose. "Planned sounds too regimented" you might say. In the traditional sense planning for something might feel like it has the potential to choke out spontaneous innovation. It's the opposite of that.

This idea can be explained by a stack of Texas ribs. Being from Texas I know that there are really only two food groups: BBQ and Tex-Mex. Most native Texans know that any good set of pork ribs have been soaked in a nice broth for a long time before they hit the grill. The meat absorbs the flavor of the broth and the result is a far more amazing rib than if you just quickly threw some salts on the rack and toss them on the fire.

> Side note: ribs make amazing LAN party food if you practice moderation - while folks are recovering from being slapped in the mouth by the killer ribs you just grilled you can get in a few extra frags.

The idea here is to take the awesome idea that you just had and make it even more awesome by soaking it in or running it by a friend or family member; then set an execution date and do it.

The best ideas are toxic without execution.

They can consume you and spit you out. Un-executed ideas will eat up your mental capital before you know it and discourage you from ever trying to do anything again. Decide early on if your idea is worth doing, then do it if it is. You could also just drop the idea of ideas all together and just start doing projects. Thinking and being more concrete will act as a catalyst to your project war machine.

What thought paradoxes turn you into the proverbial zombie? Perhaps a little soaking in the broth of planning and choice making will help keep you on the bike and help make sure you see your amazing project to its end.

The Roll For Initiative

There are tons of things that can catch us off guard in life. New perspectives, new relationships, new kids, new jobs, heck even new food can shoot your wheels off (especially if you are allergic to it). We can spend so much time on expecting the unexpected that we lose sight on one of the best and most incredible experiences in life - being surprised.

The first time I found out I was going to be a dad I had lots of new emotions to process. I remember thinking how exciting it was going to be while considering how terrifyingly unprepared we were. Even after adopting our sixth kid I was much less surprised but she still brought a stack of her own little unexpected delights.

We have a dangerous tendency to think that we have more than enough mental dexterity to anticipate life's little explosions. Combine that with the idea that fear of the unknown is paralyzing and you've got yourself one mind-blowing paradox. It's almost as if we spend loads of time preparing for something we're afraid we'll never do!

I remember building a new computer. My first experience with computing had been a TRS-80 and I was about to graduate to the 32-bit world of micro processing. It was a 386 or better known as an i386[37] packing a whopping 275,000 transistors and capable of 32-bit operations.

Running at a cool 33 MHz I thought, "what can I do with all of this power?!" Take over governments, write the Asimov predicted AI, melt faces like Indiana Jones - the possibilities were endless! Once I finished assembling the machine I flipped the switch to turn it on (literally, there was a "switch", it was red and the

---

[37] http://en.wikipedia.org/wiki/Intel_80386

"click" made a sound like a herd of unicorns dancing on a rainbow). In anticipation, I waited for the CPU to register and the memory to count up and then it happened...

BEEP...BEEP...BEEP...BEEP

Nothing but silence after that. No fans, no clicks, no BEEPs; the unicorns had fallen off the rainbow. I was now caught "flat-footed" and had failed my initiative roll. So in comes the choice every role player has to make with any encounter they have: stay and fight or run away.

The fact is that we all have these defining moments, big or small throughout life. We can choose to move the family or we can stay, we can change from a salaried employee to a contractor or just stay where we are, we can teach our kids to solder or we can decide that's too "dangerous." Regardless of the moment we all have to roll for initiative some time and we all have to decide what to do with the results. I'm not talking about a notion of chance or statistical probability but rather an opportunity to make a choice.

When rolling, fear can be a powerful factor. It can tear you down or it can be a powerful motivator. You see, when those four beeps rung in my ears I had absolutely no clue what to do or even what was next. There was no Google to help guide me through, no instructions or Geek squad. There was just me and a pile of silicon and solder. I was facing a monster and it was wielding a +4 club of hardware failure. This was my moment of adversity.

Many great individuals have been born into adverse situations, rough starts and challenged paths:

Ada Lovelace[38] dealt with an absent father and numerous health issues. It took roughly 100 years after her death for her contributions in computer science to be added to her legacy, making her the world's first computer programmer.

Bill Gates'[39], with friend Paul Allen, first company "Traf-O-Data" was initially considered unsuccessful. He later founded one of the world's largest software companies, Microsoft and is now considered one of the richest person in the world.

Stephen King's[40] first novel was rejected 30 times but then a year later was published as a huge success. He is now known around the world for his critically-acclaimed titles that have sold over 350 million copies!

Thomas Edison[41] failed many times trying numerous materials (the real number is unknown) while trying

---

[38] http://www.biography.com/people/ada-lovelace-20825323

[39] http://www.biography.com/people/bill-gates-9307520

[40] http://www.biography.com/people/stephen-king-9365136

[41] http://www.biography.com/people/thomas-edison-9284349

73

to create a new filament to make the incandescent electric light a viable device. He is now considered to have been one of America's greatest business leaders.

Vincent van Gogh[42] sold only one painting for 400 francs during his lifetime. Today he is considered to be one of the greatest Dutch painters and his paintings are some of the most expensive in the world.

Franklin Roosevelt[43] was paralyzed from polio. He led the United States through the Great Depression, World War II and has been the only president in US history to be elected to office for four terms (prior to the twenty-second amendment).

Lucille Ball[44] was known in Hollywood initially as the "queen of 'B' movies" and her childhood was filled with tragedy and money challenges. She is now remebered as one of the most beloved comedians of all time.

Stephen Hawking[45] was diagnosed at age 21 with amyotrophic lateral sclerosis (ALS). Despite his illness he has made crucial contributions to the field of physics and other sciences.

[42]http://www.biography.com/people/vincent-van-gogh-9515695
[43]http://www.biography.com/people/franklin-d-roosevelt-9463381
[44]http://www.biography.com/people/lucille-ball-9196958
[45]http://www.biography.com/people/stephen-hawking-9331710

Stan Lee[46] spent part of his childhood surviving the great depression with his parents and his younger brother. He is responsible for shaping most of what "comics" are today.

At the end of the day these people were just people like you and me. Maybe they all had a great deal of mental fortitude, perhaps they all just had a great deal of endurance but we all share something in common - the ability to make a choice regardless of the circumstances.

I chose to use the fear of the unknown and decided to use that as fuel to learn as much as I possibly could about computing, starting with four ominous beeps. Many years later I love every minute that I get a chance to write software with amazingly talented people while learning something new just about every

[46]http://www.biography.com/people/stan-lee-21101093#synopsis

day. We can sit there and think about "trying" all day long but without the "do" we're just burning a clock.

I think Yoda said it best: "There is no try there is only do and do not."

Was it because the i386 hijinks years ago or that I was obsessed with how programmers Toshihiko Nakago[47] and Kazuaki Morita at Nintendo were able to make Mario[48] jump and eat mushrooms? I don't know; it was probably a combination of several things. What I do know is that the choices we make can and will shape our lives and our family and friend's lives.

It turns out that my video card was "unseated" and all I really need to do was push it in a bit more.

I wonder if we took a step back and looked at what we are doing and considered why we are doing it would we find areas that simply need a little push to get us running like we should be running.

---

[47]http://nintendo.wikia.com/wiki/Toshihiko_Nakago
[48]http://en.wikipedia.org/wiki/Super_Mario_Bros.

The BAF

In most MMORPGs[49] there is a common term for when players round-up many mobs[50] (a computer controlled non-player character; like a monster) on accident as they are either "passing through" or "farming" for quests and the like. This term is BAF or "Bring A Friend." Often this is considered a bad thing because doing so causes unforeseen consequences. The problem is that as a PC (player character) you intend on trying to fight one thing and end up needing to fight two.

BAF is MMORPG slang for the characteristic of some computer controlled bad guys that draw aggro (attack behavior) from one or more nearby enemies to the

---

[49]http://en.wikipedia.org/wiki/Massively_multiplayer_online_role-playing_game

[50]http://en.wikipedia.org/wiki/Mob_%28video_gaming%29

character when pulled (attacked by the player). An enemy that has the behavior of bringing in more than one enemy to the player when pulled individually considered to be a "BAF mob."

A several years ago there was an extremely popular example[51] from the game World of Warcraft illustrating what can happen when the idea of "bringing a friend" goes bad.

This is how the event is described on wikipedia[52]: "The video was released by the World of Warcraft players' guild "PALS FOR LIFE". It features a group of players discussing a detailed battle strategy for the next encounter while one of their party members, Leeroy, is away from his computer. Their risky plan is needed specifically to help Leeroy, yet is ruined when Leeroy returns and, ignorant of the strategy, immediately charges headlong into battle shouting his own name in a stylized battle cry. His companions rush to help, but Leeroy's actions ruin the meticulous plan, and all of the group members are massacred."

Our friend Leeroy BAF'ed so many bad guys that he ended up flattening his group. He was ironically going in alone dragging not only the creatures around but bringing his friends in as well.

---

[51] https://www.youtube.com/watch?v=LkCNJRfSZBU
[52] http://en.wikipedia.org/wiki/Leeroy_Jenkins

This principle applies very differently in real life. In fact instead of losing levels by bringing folks in you might actually have the opportunity to level up.

A long time ago in a LAN party not so far away I learned the importance of sharing experiences and our beautiful design to create and build. There were three of us and we would start the weekend with a bike ride through back woods trails then head back to the house for some BBQ and an all nighter' of Unreal Tournament[53]. It was good fun between good friends but we grew accustomed to each other's play style and behaviors. The gatherings only started getting really interesting when we started bringing other friends into the fold. This introduced new games, new styles of game play and a new set of fun challenges. Most importantly it helped us learn and grow together as friends.

When I had my first kid, Caden, I would get frustrated that he'd get into my tools, bread boards and various RadioShack leftovers. I got frustrated because I didn't understand how principles of BAF could apply to friends and family. Once I began teaching my children how to make and contribute to the world around them, in kind, they began giving back to me. Their experience contributed to our collective experience

---

[53]https://en.wikipedia.org/wiki/Unreal_Tournament

new ways to do things and new ideas.

Enthusiasm is infectious. Passion is magnetic. We call it charisma and we assign it to a subset of humanity. We think that you have to be a great speaker or an extrovert to have that magical attribute but the fact is that **charisma is simply the ability to communicate your passion**.

We can see this no matter where we are or who we are around. If you love what you're doing it will most likely ooze from your pores. The idea is simple: "Begin a movement by just being you." I no longer tell my kids that we are going to do a project over the coming weekend; they now either bring me project ideas or I'll catch them in the middle of their own make.

Over the years I have had many friends look at me oddly as I spoke vibrantly about something I loved. I could generally write it off as I just look funny and they are giving me an appropriate response to that. As I dug in more and more I discovered that what was going on was something extraordinary. The contorted looks were coming from them processing an infection. It's like this:

A friend tells you that you have to try dipping your fries in your vanilla shake. To you the mere thought of dipping the crispy goodness of those tasty treats into anything other than your face makes you sad. Your friend persists and you can tell they are speaking from a position of enthusiasm and you begin wondering if there is something to what they are saying. Finally you find yourself doing what you never thought you would and you take the proverbial plunge into "shake fry fishing." You taste and you are well pleased. In fact you are so delighted that you begin telling others about this amazing transcendence. This is how we process infectious passion. Sometimes it doesn't catch and sometimes it does. The amazingly cool thing about passion is that it does not have to have a reason; it's its own reason.

Each of us have a stockpile of life experience. The pile often looks nothing like what we set out to build when we started our life but it is a beautiful disaster of experiences that are unique to you and no one else. We can choose to hold onto this collection and let it collect dusk like old MTG (Magic the Gathering) cards or we can use them in a game with others where we can learn and grow and help others do the same.

I started playing MTG[54] in the early 90's. As I collected the cards, I used them. It was easy to spend an hour or so opening up a single booster pack. It was the smell of the mint condition cards, the feel of the prints in my hands and of course the beautiful content (art and

[54]https://en.wikipedia.org/wiki/Magic:_The_Gathering

writing) that made time stop. With every pack a whole new experience was waiting for me; an opportunity to create new decks and new experiences for others. This was not unique to Magic the Gathering. I had the same experience with baseball cards years earlier.

We place a tremendous amount of value on inanimate things and trading cards are no exception. Is it the beautiful art work or the value of the thing or player on the cards? I don't think so; at least not entirely. For example, in the card game, Magic the Gathering, there is an extremely valuable card that has been known to sell for $125,000 signed! That's six figures! At first glance the card looks normal and perhaps uninterest-ing. It is also now banned in most tournaments so the card is virtually unusable. So why the high sticker value? It's because the card has "experience value."

Allow me to explain a bit about how the Magic the Gathering game works. Players build decks with a minimum of forty cards (in a tournament) or sixty in normal play. Game play is one to many and like any game there is a set of concrete rules and a set of "respect" rules that are simply followed for good etiquette.

Everyone starts the game with twenty life and the basic goal of the game is to get the opposing player or players down to 0 before you. You do this by using an amazingly robust set of cards that span the MTG universe. The card types include creature, artifact, enchantments, land (also known as mana - the currency of the game) and so on. In MTG mana is everything.

There is a collection of early series cards in the game called the power 9[55]. These are considered to be the most powerful / valuable cards in the game and one of them has the six figure price tag mentioned above: the Black Lotus. Six of those nine cards were mana generators that can give a tremendous amount of power to any player. I mentioned the core goal of the game was to reduce your opposing player's life to zero. The Black Lotus allowed you to do this in the very first turn of the game. Here's how it worked:

---

[55]http://en.wikipedia.org/wiki/Power_Nine

At the beginning of the game each player draws seven cards. You only needed four cards to help you execute this amazing combo: a mountain land, Fireball, Channel and of course the Black Lotus. On your turn, you can play a single land. You would play the Mountain, and then put your Black Lotus out for zero mana. Lands do not have summoning sickness[56], so you are able to use land and artifacts when you play them.

You then would use the Black Lotus[57], which will give you three green mana. Cast Channel[58] and make 19 of your own life into 19 "colorless" mana. You now have that 19 colorless, one red and one green mana (from the Black Lotus) in your pool. "Tap" or use the mountain and cast Fireball[59], which costs one red mana and X, where X is the number of mana. Take the 19 extra mana and add it to fireball and then add the last green mana still in your pool for a twenty damage Fireball. Game over, you win.

Now that you've recovered from MTG overload you're probably wondering "why all of the detail, I've never played MTG nor do I intend on ever playing." I described it this way to set up an experience. Can

[56]http://mtg.wikia.com/wiki/Summoning_Sickness

[57]http://gatherer.wizards.com/Pages/Card/Details.aspx?multiverseid=382866

[58]http://gatherer.wizards.com/Pages/Card/Details.aspx?name=channel

[59]http://gatherer.wizards.com/Pages/Card/Details.aspx?multiverseid=393831

you imagine the excitement, the adrenaline, the sheer intensity of being the player that draws this combo for the first time! What if you're a Tekken[60], Mortal Combat[61] or Street fighter[62] player and you pull a combo that is only known as "technically" being possible? What if you have been working on a 3D model for months and it printed correctly on the first try? What about solving the unsolved algorithm?

The Black Lotus is valuable because of the emotion and excitement it brings to a situation. It can drive a normal experience to one of extreme splendor.

Card	Value (from mtgprice.com as of 2015)	Card text (courtesy of Wizards of the Coast)
Black Lotus	$17,000.00[63]	Sacrifice Black Lotus: Add three mana of any one color to your mana pool.
Time Walk	$3,200.00[64]	Take an extra turn after this one.

[60]http://en.wikipedia.org/wiki/Tekken

[61]http://en.wikipedia.org/wiki/Mortal_Kombat

[62]http://en.wikipedia.org/wiki/Street_Fighter

[63]http://www.mtgprice.com/sets/Alpha/Black_Lotus

[64]http://www.mtgprice.com/sets/Alpha/Time_Walk

Card	Value (from mtgprice.com as of 2015)	Card text (courtesy of Wizards of the Coast)
Ancestral Recall	$4,160.00[65]	Target player draws three cards.
Mox Sapphire	$4,160.00[66]	Add Island,to your mana pool.
Mox Jet	$2,873.00[67]	Add Swamp,to your mana pool.
Mox Ruby	$2,849.00[68]	Add Mountain,to your mana pool.
Mox Pearl	$2,600.00[69]	Add Plains,to your mana pool.
Mox Emerald	$2,849.00[70]	Add Forrest,to your mana pool.

---

[65] http://www.mtgprice.com/sets/Alpha/Ancestral_Recall

[66] http://www.mtgprice.com/sets/Alpha/Mox_Sapphire

[67] http://www.mtgprice.com/sets/Alpha/Mox_Jet

[68] http://www.mtgprice.com/sets/Alpha/Mox_Ruby

[69] http://www.mtgprice.com/sets/Alpha/Mox_Pearl

[70] http://www.mtgprice.com/sets/Alpha/Mox_Emerald

Card	Value (from mtgprice.com as of 2015)	Card text (courtesy of Wizards of the Coast)
Timetwister	$1,822.00[71]	Each player shuffles his or her hand and graveyard into his or her library, then draws seven cards.

I've been blessed to see some of the most amazing accomplishments in my career. At a place like New Relic this type of thing happens often: discovery, innovation, breakthroughs and doing the impossible are an ear mark of sorts for the people I get to work with. The halls are filled regularly with "You've got to see this!"

It's the experiences that make us want to run around the room throwing high fives and people have a built-in desire to be a part of that. Bringing your friends and family to join you in making and creating new things emboldens the experience. Will you need to buy a new hammer on occasion because the kids left yours outside? Sure you will. Will you get a chance to see the

[71]http://www.mtgprice.com/sets/Alpha/Timetwister

little ones you love so much have an amazing amount of delight when they find a Black lotus in what they built? Absolutely!

Accept that things will not go as planned and that stuff will break.

So how will you BAF the next time you're doing something you're excited about?

The Behavior Parables

It seems that we, as the human race, have several different opinions or ideas of what "success" means. Whether it's working one hundred hours a week to pull off the amazing project or, like me, taking every opportunity to teach my kids the how's and what's of the things I am passionate about, we all have a perspective. Maybe it's our perceived ideal. Regardless, there is a definition of what we think we should pursue and often times we are willing to fall on many swords to get there.

Game theory[72] defines our tendency to sprint toward certain behaviors like this:

> "The more 'successful' behaviors tend to be held more tenaciously and will occur more frequently."

Basically, if you do x and a positive result comes of it, you'll continue to do x. This is considered to be reinforcement learning[73]. It suggests that we will stop doing something else in favor of the thing that is making us "successful." There are a few potential stumbling blocks that many of us could face with this type of behavioral realignment.

First, we sometimes allow outside influences to direct our idea of "success." Perhaps it was a college professor, your parents, a spouse, or your coworkers that began laying the bricks in your road to winning. Before you know it you're trying to fulfill someone else's dream or hopes.

*   *   *

[72]http://en.wikipedia.org/wiki/Game_theory
[73]http://en.wikipedia.org/wiki/Reinforcement_learning

It was the third night in a row he was at work, trying to keep up with the shear workload. Overwhelmed by commitments and to-dos. "How did I get here" he thought. The pressure was intense; so much so that the work became blurry and he was treading water by mashing random keys on the keyboard.

He was going nowhere as a result of being told where to go. A week earlier, his boss came in and told him that the upcoming project was going to be critical in determining if he was going to "move up." He pondered his days in college and remembered that it seemed like a continual crunch and that his professors always said that he'd be successful. "If a constant push in overdrive worked then, surely it will work now..."

This was not the first time this type of carrot had been dangled in front of him or his coworkers. Incrementally he moved through the organization and did well there. All that he had to pay was 100 hour weeks, several anxiety ridden nights, his health and of course his family. Years later, as he looked back over his shoulder, he did not feel very successful when he saw that he had lost everything except his job.

*   *   *

This is a tight loop we all have the potential to get stuck in. Often, many of us can do our jobs really well and we can "succeed" in doing them with precision. *Winning feels good, losing feels bad.* In the confidence we have we can visualize what success means to us and apply that to our day jobs. The computer programmer might say that her job is not rocket science, the rocket scientist might say his job is not particle physics and the physicist might say their job isn't as complex as parenting.

I've discovered that there is a correlation to things that are challenging to maintain but highly valuable, such as friendships or marriages. The problem is that because there are unknown factors in things like relationships they can become daunting but tremendously rewarding. These variables make it extraordinarily difficult to solve for x. On the other side things like working a lot has the potential to yield frequent, smaller rewards that are often assured - looking back to the idea of the Skinner effect.

What if what we thought was success was wrong? What if we are basing our definition of winning on a lifetime ago where the only thing we had to think about was how long of a car nap you could take before your next class?

I'd like to take a minute and look at some of the influencers and behaviors that create these ideal pictures of what we think winning looks like. Keep in mind that these things are not inherently bad per se (much like the money point in a previous chapter), but that what we do with them can create the not so favorable scenarios.

Once you're done going through some of these behavior parables ask yourself, what behaviors have been reinforced in the way you work and interact with the world around you. Do those behaviors still seem successful to you now?

The Death Of A Tauntan

In the Star Wars universe there are creatures known as Tauntans. These omnivores are indigenous to the planet Hoth. Hoth is a super cold planet that is almost uninhabitable save the creatures who called it home and the rebels that were trying to rebuild and regroup on it.

The rebels used these creatures as patrol mounts to travel across the surface of Hoth because their vehicles couldn't cope with the cold.

As it would turn out as the story unfolds there are limitations to the Tauntans as well. Han Solo runs one into the ground looking for Luke, then proceeds to make a sleeping bag out of it to help our hero get "Luke-warm."

Have you ever caught yourself saying something like, "Once this project is over things will get back to 'normal'?" We do that because our vision is "siloed" in on a fixed point. We do some self-encouraging as we run hard we take a breath and we start running again. The "skinner effect" is invoked and we find ourselves getting kited along until we are drinking energy drinks and coffee every morning and finishing the day with a dose of melatonin just to stop our brains from spinning.

Keep in mind I am not talking about crunch, there will always be that. There will always be times when we have a hack that we need to get out of our head and turn into code or an idea that needs a weekend and half a dozen trips to Home Depot to get done. I think we all have a tendency to be a bit hardheaded which can be a strength to help us persevere. No, I'm not talking about that at all; it is the patterns where we cannot walk away despite the project or activity. It's obsession.

Think of it like this: You decide that you really have a fondness for cats. You can debate quite effectively that they are the sole purpose the Internet was invented, you can quickly cite amazing facts about them and they are the topic of every one of your conversations. You have now effectively removed 2-dimensions from your character. Your friends seem to fade away and even your cats think you a bit odd. You are consumed. You get to the end of your life and you realize cleaning cat boxes and hairballs wasn't really all that and end up regretting the time lost.

That Is what obsession can look like and it has the

ability to rob you of many amazing years. If you find yourself sandwiching your days between energy drinks and melatonin tablets you might want to stop and check what "winning" really looks like to you because you might simply be stuck in a tight loop and eventually you're going to run out of memory and drop dead.

Never once in my career has being away from my family, friends or hobbies ever made anyone fonder of me or me of them. The absurdity of either spending more time physically or mentally at a place called "work" is really deceiving. From the outside, it looks like a developer is killing "it" during those late nights and weekends. I get some of my best software ideas just chatting with my kids about things completely unrelated to software or technology. Being around those I love helps me be more creative.

The type of thinking about the need to work long hours is dangerous because it is deceiving and can end up killing you. I tend to use Judge Dredd, the movie as an example when I bring this bad behavior up. In the movie, there was a family named the Angel Gang and one of the "gang" was named "Mean Machine" Angel who was a cyborg who had an adjustable dial on his head ranging from 1, where he is like an ill-tempered sea bass, up to 4, where he goes berserk. As the movie progresses, this family captures Judge

Dredd and the "Mean Machine's" dial is turned all the way up. Eventually, the cyborg's head explodes because he was pushing an "extreme" level far too long - that's what could happen to us; we will burn out and it could be far worse than simply being tired.

Secondly, this behavior deceives your team and establishes the unrealistic expectation that your projects will always be done in an accelerated time frame, which will eventually become the expected norm.

Third, it deceives you. I know firsthand that burnout will occur and your ability to perform will diminish. We cannot always run as energy drink-infused developers if we want to continue to deliver great software.

Finally, overworked people often end up changing crafts. There is an economic law, the law diminishing marginal utility[74], which states that if you increase the consumption of something (keeping all other things constant) you will eventually lose interest in the thing you consume. Consider a food buffet: the first plate of food is awesome but each subsequent plate drives you deeper into misery and begins to look more like regret than food.

---

[74]http://www.investopedia.com/terms/l/lawofdiminishingutility.asp

"In Return of the Jedi, Jabba the Hutt has a stuffed and mounted tauntaun head as one of his grisly trophies, right next to the frozen form of Han Solo." Makes you wonder if it was the tauntaun Han shot first. source: starwars.wikia.com[a]

---

[a] http://starwars.wikia.com/wiki/Tauntaun

The Costco Mentality

So you walk into your favorite bulk retailer / warehouse outlet and some of the first things you'll run into are the sample ninjas. These people are highly skilled at getting you to: 1. eat crap off a table you had no hand in preparing and 2. make you want to buy said crap so that you and your family can become addicted to a veritable cornucopia of deathly delights.

Unwittingly places like Costco allow my family in the doors. You see, my children are like locusts (I am sure any parents with pre-teens and up can relate); they leave in their paths little paper cups and worn out sample ninjas.

Sometimes the mentality of a nerd can be the little locust running through the store. We consume a little of the latest programming language, the most recent build of an OS, the next great cloud service and we leave in the wake little half-done projects or bits and pieces of provisioned websites. As the sampling continues we ping the moderators of the frameworks or projects we nibble on and talk about how great feature x and y would be and then turn around and abandon all interest in it because a new thing was put in front of us.

Sampling is not a bad thing at all. Trying out new things can help you learn, grow, develop skills and make you question the status quo. It's just that if all we do is sample we'll never actually get any thing done. Next time you stroll through the Costco of your field or interest remember to set some "try" constraints for yourself so that you can actually put a meal on the table.

The retailer Costco sells more than 43 million packages of toilet paper every year. So keep eating those samples, they've got you covered. source: Costco facebook[a]

---

[a] https://www.facebook.com/Costco

Infinite Planning

Planning is good. It helps us avoid things like project bloat, confusion and give us a general direction to head in. A few years back I began a project with my kids. It was a "zipline." The problems we were trying to solve were simple:

1. Have a faster way to get from the house to a trail head. At the time we had a really big yard and my kids legs are short.
2. Build something fun and safe for the family to enjoy

So, like most projects we do together we all sat down and began to plan. We were drawing up plans and calculating for tension and sag. About 5 minutes I lost my two-year old, an hour into it my four-year old dropped out because of boredom, another hour I lost the five-year old to "chores" (interesting how boredom can be a motivator), and finally roughly 30 minutes later my 7 and 9 year olds stopped the "planning" with one simple question: "Why are we doing this? It doesn't seem like we're actually getting anything done."

Then it hit me: When you gold plate everything you end up with absolutely nothing. Weâ€¦ I was gold plating the plan. Two years later we still had no zipline until one day I see my now 2 years older kid spin by me in a flurry with one of his belts. Past incidents had taught me to investigate, so I followed him out the door. There is was in all of its glory, a makeshift zipline. They had found some old tension cable that I had from another project and pulled it between two trees. As he raced down the line, belt in hand, I realized that it's not failure when you plant seeds. Two years later he was inspired, using his own design, to build what I failed to plan. For all you parents, take opportunities to dream big with your kids because eventually they will make new, better dreams out of that which we thought was impossible. Just try to time box the conversation so that you don't gold plate your way into a two-year delay.

The drive for perfection is unfortunately a journey to insanity. Plain and simple, constantly tweaking something without delivering is a developer's pit of despair.

Ironically, we do this to ourselves because we love our perfect lines, application richness and the mental game of crafting fake criticism.

I've been down this road far too many times - I

have even gold-plated specifications and documents! The part in every maker, developer, craft person that makes what we do so amazing is that we love to dream. We need to learn how to stop trying to "live the dream" and start iterating on it.

> *"Volo dell angelo Zipline located in Rocca Massima, Italy is the longest Zipline in the world clocking in at a whopping 2,213 meters or 7,260 feet! Riders can reach speeds of 140 km/h." *
> source: Flying in the Sky[a]
>
> ---
> [a]http://www.flyinginthesky.it/

The Steam Powered Punch

At the time of this writing there is a movement where boxed software and games have moved to an unboxed downloadable content (DLC) model. This approach has gained rapid approval because of the accessibility to users and their content, creator to user reach and it has opened the door to many creators who simply cannot work in the publisher / creator model. Basically you can buy, download content and play within minutes. It's ingenious, at least as a business model. For those of us who have collector mentalities it becomes a bit of a challenge because when things go on sale in this market place we tend to buy games we probably will never play. If you have a Steam account how many of the games in your library have you actually played? 50%? 30%? 10%?

The idea here is that there is a lot of things that desire our attention and there typically is a lot to be done. We need to learn to sift through the rocks to find the gold. Find the best "farming" spot in our lives. We sometimes need to give up the **good** to experience the

great.

> *"In the game Half-life, the first game built by Valve Software, artillery bombardments occur frequently throughout the game. The 'whistling' sound that can be heard before the explosion is that of the German Flak 88."* source: IMDB [a]

[a] http://www.imdb.com/title/tt0239023/trivia

Taking A Quantum Leap

I couldn't figure it out and the problem was filling my head like tribbles on a starship. After working for a month on a caching solution for a web application I was doing, I felt no closer to the ideal solution then when I started.

Often times software developers will refer to the "two hardest problems in software." It's adage that refers to:

1. Naming things in your projects
2. Caching invalidation strategy that will help performance and reduce the normal operating overhead of their applications.

These things are referred to "the hardest things in computer science" for a good reason:

1. Naming stuff is challenging, especially if others are involved

2. As a good curator of software you want to
   create a solution that will not end up being
   the Rube Goldburg[75] of cache invalidation solutions.

*   *   *

I was WFH (working from home) one day and I simply
put my hands to my face and let out a pretty pitiful
sigh. My seven year old at the time heard my anguish
and asked what was wrong.

> "Nothing kiddo, I'm just trying to figure
> something out."

> "Tell me, I can help."

We've built a culture of fearlessly sharing in my
house. I call it the "know nothing" principle. Much
like Occam's razor, it's an attempt to draw out the
obvious by asking the impossible. We ask questions in
our house to simultaneously learn for ourselves and to

---

[75] http://en.wikipedia.org/wiki/Rube_Goldberg

make others think. I am sure most everyone practices this on some level.

Knowing that I have not taught him the principles of caching in coding yet, I distilled the problem to a few basic concepts and explained those to him. His response was astonishing. He said, "How do you know you need to do that [use caching]?" I was speechless. He single-handedly unwound all of my preconceived notions about the project and the gold plating I was apparently doing.

It turns out that my assumptions about the need for caching the data I was caching were completely wrong for this project and it was not needed. If I had of compartmentalized my work and life I would've ended up missing out on a lesson my son was giving me on critical thinking. I would also miss out on the moment where my son solved one of the most challenging questions in computer science.

*   *   *

I have found that attempting to turn off life at work and work at life is often frustrating. Most developers are probably continually mentally working to resolve questions about how their environment works or how to transform a slow process into a faster one.

Being at work does not throw a life switch nor does being home involve throwing a work switch. Think of this as more of a circuit without a switch: your passion is the power source and work and life are the wires that are attached to what you want to accomplish or do. Instead of having your work ideas compartmentalized why not try talking about them with your friends and family - you might be surprised what happens. Talk to someone at work about things going on in your life. I always wondered when having a personality that you wanted to share at work became taboo; share it, you might find that you might have more in common than just code.

This idea is often misunderstood as: "you're saying think about work all the time" or "I should bring work home and push other stuff to the side?" Not at all! I'm simply pointing out that your inner nerd components, whether it's code, bikes, writing, weight lifting or whatever, are part of you; they should be expressed and shared. It will inherently be part of what you love to do and talk about.

Just like a coin has two functional sides to be valid currency, we also have these sides as "nerds" that we need to validate as our life currency - find out what your currencies are, share them and watch the excitement spread like wildfire.

The point is that we can easily miss the whole picture by trying to be a quantum person. Try treating work and life more like Velcro and less like sand paper. You might find that you have a lot to learn from your family and friends.

> *"Scott Bakula ad libbed the line "Oh boy!" at the end of an episode of Quantum Leap. The producer liked it so much that it became the signature final line of each episode, as Sam finds himself in a new body."* source: IMDB[a]

[a]http://www.imdb.com/title/tt0096684/trivia

Impostor

You're starting a new job today. With the new adventure comes loads of excitement, stress, an opportunity to learn something new and perhaps an opportunity to get schooled. Then it happens; the excitement turns to dread. The people you are working with seem to have a Matrix like ability to "jack in" and do anything while you're still working in bullet time. They are making a difference while you fill out docs for Human resources.

Let's turn off our emotional roller coasters for a minute and reflect. You made it through the interview, the team hopefully likes you and they wouldn't have hired you unless you had something to offer.

The quickest way to being perceived as an impostor is to act like one. Acting "sketchy" is one way to earn your impostor badge. Communicating with partial information, flip-flopping and even exhibiting an always agreeable mode will come across as nonsense.

Another way is to act with hubris. Being prideful or boastful is one of the quickest ways to discredit yourself and your abilities. Let your "yes" be "yes" and your "no" be "no." There is absolute beauty in respecting simplicity. Can you imagine how much we could get done if we all simply practiced saying, "I don't know."

Here's the crux: When you are comparing yourself and your skills to other people you are doing yourself and your team a disservice. You're putting your eyes on you instead of on what needs to be done. Have you ever told yourself "I'll never be good enough?" Let me let you in on a little secret: you're right. You see, if you constantly put your sights on what everyone else can do how will you ever know what you can do? You are jumping for a block you cannot hit, Mario. Try breaking your own blocks.

I often ask myself who defines "good enough" and when I ask that question I often find that it is me who sets the bar and sometimes it's based on what others can do.

As a side note, if you are an impostor, one of the best and most risky thing you can do is talk to your boss or friend and let them know you want to seek opportunities to learn and grow where you are. You also might be in the wrong place and you simply need to get in the right place to thrive. We have too few hours on this earth to spend them doing something we really have no interest in doing.

"Frank Abagnale began his career in fraud at age 15. His known impersonations were an airline pilot, a doctor, an attorney and even a teaching assistant." source: wikipedia[a]

---

[a] http://en.wikipedia.org/wiki/Frank_Abagnale

The Pain Of Sand

You're on a beach, the sun is out and the waves are crashing. It's a beautiful day. You build sand castles with the kids and when you're done you decide to go for a quick run. Halfway through your run you realize you have several grains of sand in your britches and all of the running and rubbing has caused you a seriously painful rash.

One or two grains of sand in your life can quickly become a painfully searing rash. Most likely we spend more time in the environment of our craft than we do sleeping. If your work bench is in disarray, your developer IDE settings work against you, your office layout makes you stumble or if your home school setup causes your eye to twitch rather than spend time teaching you might have a problem.

Like most learned things we will naturally begin to avoid the painful things in our environment. In terms of the small irritating things in our environments these can be grains of sand that can add up quickly and begin to irritate on a massive scale. I call this the **grain of sand factor**. It is the idea that over time if we do not address the small irritants in our lives quickly that overtime the net result is that they will be really expensive to deal with and could drive us away from what we love to do.

The following are two representations of this grain of sand thinking. Even though this line of thinking is spelled out using a contrived algorithm the principle is somewhat simple: know when to stop and address something that is irritating you and distracting you from getting real work done.

The Bad Grain

$$time = \sum_{i=1}^{n} [(grain_i) * (N + times\ it\ comes\ up_i)]$$

The Good Grain

$$time = \sum_{i=1}^{n} [(grain_i) * (time\ to\ fix_i)]$$

Shake the sand out as frequently as possible. I've been blessed to have the opportunity to mentor many developers and I generally tell them,

> "A good developer knows how to shake the sand out, a great developer knows when to shake it out."

Accept that there will be times when you'll have to take the sand but know when it's time to shake out and clean house.

"To make the location perfect for shooting, two hundred workers spent two months hand-clearing three-square miles of Mexican desert for the epic 1984 film Dune. " source: inktank[a]

[a]http://inktank.fi/15-little-known-facts-about-the-making-of-dune

Talking About Things

There is an old proverb that states: "Silence is golden." The origin of this is still uncertain however there are instances of this thought appearing in ancient Egypt, in the Judaic Biblical commentaries (the Midrash), the English poet Thomas Carlyle referenced it, James Russell Lowell quotes it in 'The Bigelow Papers', in Brian Aldiss' 'The Primal Urge' and even William Shakespeare tips his hat to the thought in "Romeo and Juliet."

If you are a parent, most likely you have used a form or version of this with your kids. What a paradox our children are! I find it amazing and sometimes painful that they are continually sharing their stream of consciousness it an audible form as if they are compelled by something. I think we can learn something from how our kids do this.

My theory is the reason that they are talking nonstop is that they are simply processing the universe. Something that I feel that we as adults have sadly "grayed out." If we stop, unplug from our "i-tether" and look around at the whole of creation I am sure eventually we will begin describing its amazing design to our friends and family. We will be as children, trying to take in the creativity of it all.

As people who write software, cross stitch, build computers, generate art we owe it to ourselves to plug-out and plug-in to life around us. Talk out loud to others and ourselves.

This is one of the reasons I feel we should take our passions "home" with us. By talking what you love to your friends and family you open up opportunities to share some thing you love while building relationships that are lasting. If we genuinely love what we do we will have this burning desire to share it. Think about the times when you are working on something tough or thinking through an idea you have. Do you talk to yourself? Perhaps you talk to your pets or inanimate objects. While some might consider talking to one's self the beginnings of schizophrenia many feel that it's a way for logically processing the complexities of what we do.

In the Half-Life series of video games created by Valve the main protagonist Gordon Freeman never says a single word. "Gabe Newell has stated[a] that Valve sees no reason to give Gordon

*a voice." I suppose if I had a crowbar talking
for me I wouldn't need a voice either.* source:
wikipedia[b]

---

[a]http://www.computerandvideogames.com/241221/gabe-
newell-next-half-life-wont-change-gordon-freeman/

[b]http://en.wikipedia.org/wiki/Gordon_Freeman

The Board Of Directors

I had been haunted by a dream where I solved a super hard problem that I had faced for about a month. The problem was seriously challenging and it was constantly hanging over my head drilling holes in my subconscious so it was not unusual that I would have a dream about it. In fact I had many dreams but this was the first time I'd "solved" it in the dream; usually the dream was knowing that the problem existed but I had to solve an equally as hard problem like naming something or caching before I could get to it.

Like most dreams the solution eluded me and I decided to place my tablet next to my bed so that when I did get the dream again I could capture it. This problem was chewing me up.

I had the dream again and with delight I opened my eyes and attempted to cast a "root" on it. I turned on my tablet, almost missed my pass code 3 times (if I'd missed it the 3rd time I would've resorted to paper - I was that desperate), opened up my email and began drafting what was going to be the most epic solution - it possibly would even cure all diseases and world hunger. I finished and I mashed send and passed back out, elated that it was finished.

The next day I woke expectantly to an inbox of joy, there it was the message I sent myself. Incidentally if you have a propensity to solve hard problems using dreams and care to jot them down, may I suggest you not use email? Miraculously I received my email, but as you might have guessed it was not exactly what I had intended to send. But let me not tip my hand just yet, as River Song would say "careful, no spoilers."

I had inadvertently added folks to the "To" and combined with auto correct hijinks and an obvious sleep deprived conscious I had the makings for an email sent from Benny Hill[76] of the Matrix. Interwoven with code there were double entendres and unfortunate adjectives sprinkled about. It was a veritable cornucopia of embarrassment. Oh and absolute shocker, it did not solve the problem.

When I got to work, where I spent most of the day avoiding HR, a few of the folks had passed the email

---

[76]http://en.wikipedia.org/wiki/Benny_Hill

around and were getting some enjoyment from it. While I was eating my humble pie someone asked me, "So what's the problem you've been working on?" With an expectant sigh I showed him the thing that had captivated my attention and dreams. To which he replied, "oh yeah I've seen this before." My first thought was "impossible," who would keep the solution to world hunger and my software problem to themselves!

As he took me through the solution I realized a few things:

1. The answer was literally feet away
2. I should never send sleep induced emails
3. No one asked me to try to solve this on my own. Ever.

*   *   *

In the middle of the night you always seem to have the best ideas but when you wake up you realize you were trying to fix your software with unicorns and gummy bears. Know the benefits of taking issues to your team and friends. Have a personal board of directors; people that share your passion and craft that you can count on to filter your insanity.

*"In the 1987 film "Robocop" the Desert Eagle
Magnum that is in the OCP Board Room was
originally intended to be Robocop's gun. There
is even existing behind-the-scene photos and
footage of Peter Weller practicing with the Desert
Eagle. However, when they gave Weller the gun,
they noticed that even the bulky Desert Eagle was too small in the hands of Robocop. So
the film's armory supervisor, Randy E. Moore,
brought in a Berretta Automatic Pistol to which a
compensator and decorative dressing was added
to increase the size of the gun." If one of your
personal board members carries either of those
guns you should probably listen to them!* source:
imdb[a]

---

[a]http://www.imdb.com/title/tt0093870/trivia

Going Mental

Mental illness in the work place and at home is a really serious problem that this modern workforces faces today. Sadly very little is discussed about it and often those being challenged by problems have limited outlets for fear of being cast out with a label.

The fact is that most of us have crossed paths with this at one time or another. Stress is a form of mental illness, though temporary, it can cause both psychological and physiological damage. We have a tendency to try to act strong when we are terrified on the inside. It could be that we don't want to appear weak or perhaps we don't want to face a label but whatever the case is, ignoring it can and will cause problems.

A few years back I was building an epic sandbox for my kids in our backyard in Texas. Texas has a very unique soil, some call it clay I call it brimstone. Part of the project required that I get a 2 1/4 PVC pipe and hammer it into the ground. I didn't have a sledge-hammer but I did have a 40lb dumbbell that I could swing like one.

You might have guessed that it did not go well. My last swing slightly missed the pipe and with indiscriminate justice I severed an inch off of my right index finger and severely damaged my right middle finger as well. In the following weeks I soon realized that I was going to have to relearn how to type, how to grip as well as many other things I had simply taken for granted. This took a toll on me because I thought that I had lost the ability to do what I felt I was designed to do. My tools felt broken and I felt lost. Fortunately I had (and still have) an amazing wife and group of scrappy kids to support me and take me through re-imagining what I already knew - that it was going to be OK and I will just write software a little different now.

There are many out there that do not have a support system. If you see your coworker or friend struggling, instead of ignoring the anguish on their face reach out to them and ask them how they are doing. I'm not talking about the hollow "Hey how's it going?" Let me give you a booster for conversation since many of us might be introverts:

> You: "Hey how's it going?"
>
> Friend: "Ok, I guess."
>
> You: "No, really how are you doing?"

I know this is a hard thing for us to do, we are heads down in whatever we are doing, we have our own problems, we are struggling in our own ways but we owe it to humanity to be better than what is expected of us.

We don't have to be heroes we simply need to be human.

Reaching out to others in need not only has the power to help someone in need but it has the power to change the world.

> *"People with OCD have insight, meaning they are aware that their unwanted thoughts are unreasonable. People with OCPD think their way is the "right and best way" and usually feel comfortable with such self-imposed systems of rules." Take opportunities to help yourself and others and learn more about common personality types.* source: International OCD foundation[a]

---

[a]http://iocdf.org/wp-content/uploads/2014/10/OCPD-Fact-Sheet.pdf

The End Is The Beginning

5...4...3...2...1... this is the end.

At least that's what I thought as my heart was still trying to recover from the stimpack injection from almost having someone call finalize[77] on me. I woke to challenge an on coming car in the left lane and a train and a ditch on my right.

Do you remember? I was just coming back from an all night deployment were I thought I was being exceptional and doing everything I could to "succeed" at a job where I was not happy (mostly my own doing); physically destroying myself for the illusion

---

[77]https://msdn.microsoft.com/en-us/library/system.object.finalize(v=vs.110).aspx

of being passionate about building software.

It's strange how coming so close to running out of those little hearts in the upper right hand corner of life's screen makes you stop and consider the absurdity of a situation. What is it about a dirt nap that drives us to wake up and dig our way out? Why can't we have that clarity without risking death and dismemberment?

Life asks so much from each of us.

We all go through our own trials and tribulations. We all have broken hearts and misaligned expectations. Despite all of that we all still have an opportunity to make a choice. I made that choice and I continue to make that choice every day.

What is the choice? I'll get to that in a bit. Right now let me tell you how the story ends...

As you might have already guessed I did not die that day and I did not give up on software. In fact part of me came alive. I pulled over onto the shoulder to deal with what just happened. Silence. Confusion. Terror. You know those moments in life were you playback sweaty palm events, editing and replaying how it could have gone? These are the moments when time stops and you continue to shoot adrenaline into your heart with each new version of what could've been. Even now as I relive the multitude of ways I could've left this earth I'm anxious. I really shouldn't be anxious though, last time I checked the mortality rate is still 100%, funeral homes are big business and frankly I should be putting my hope in a more important place.

I thought of the many, many times that I both put my life at risk as well as the lives of those around me for something that seemed so important. Then I began asking my self one simple question:

"Am I doing what I was created to do?" Surely I was not just here to put my carbon foot print in the dirt then leave, right?

What are the important things to you? Your friends, your kids, your spouse, cooking a great meal, going to church, writing code, traveling, making an impact?

I began biking to work shortly after we moved to Portland, OR. This was a whole new experience for me because you simply would never commute on a bike in Dallas ,TX. The heat and the Frogger[78] like road conditions alone were more than enough to keep a pedestrian or bike off the road.

I had some amazing bike nerds from New Relic backing me up with my new 24 mile round trip adventure. As a side bar I truly feel that's what we should be

---

[78]https://en.wikipedia.org/wiki/Frogger

doing throughout our life: encouraging each other in our uncertainties and sharing what we love to do.

I hated it. Bottom line I was a terrible biker, never mind that there was absolutely no good reason for me to be biking to work given the multitude of commuting options available to me in the great bridge city.

It was like taking a person who has played first person shooters (driving to work) their entire life and telling them they could now only play massively multiplayer online games (bike to work). Frankly, it seemed about as smart and as useful as a bag of broken hammers in Donkey Kong[79].

I continued to do it because:

1. I was being encouraged by some amazing people
2. I noticed something on the faces and in the hearts of the other bikers on my commute.

It was subtle initially but it really became clear when I was riding in a heavy rain. The commuters were smiling. Crazy, yes. Nutty, I know right?! They were riding on the same path I was on and in the same rain! So what was it? What made these people enjoy it so much?

---

[79]https://en.wikipedia.org/wiki/Donkey_Kong

I continued riding and I purposefully paid more attention. It's going to sound cliché but **I intentionally made it about the journey and not the destination.** It's like grinding wombats in a game to get the "crown of unsightly behavior" or something like it. We get so locked in on the prize we forget to make getting it fun.

Riding down the Springwater Corridor[80] there were expansive fields of flowers that looked like a freshly painted Monet. There was the Willamette river and the "eights" or boats filled with rowers sliding along the river as if they were on glass. There were homeless camps were I took the chance to sit down with some amazing folks and chat about life in Oregon. There were deer that raced down the train track with me and an amusement park where the cheers of a hundred voices made me ride faster as if they were cheering me on!

There was beauty everywhere and a million experiences to be had and all I had to do was stop and smell the metaphorical roses.

Then it happened. I had a smile on my face. Was it a touchy feely moment? Not at all. It happened when I caught a light rail track with my front wheel and I flew over my handlebars. I was laying on my back thinking about how I now understand why the signs

---

[80]https://en.wikipedia.org/wiki/Springwater_Corridor

with the guy falling off the bike were not really that funny after all.

Then it hit me. **I smile when I write code!** It turns out that when you are genuinely passionate about something two very interesting things happen:

1. You have tons of joy doing what your passionate about
2. You want to share it with anyone who will listen

The fact is that your passion does not need to have a reason for existing - it is its own reason. I went on to share my crazy excitement about commuting to work with whoever would listen. I was leaking excitement and passion everywhere like Ninja Turtle ooze, hoping for a mutation here or there.

You see your passion is a virus and you are patient zero. Though this virus is vastly different from any other virus in the world and it is distinct and unique. You are the only one who can "carry" it and when it infects someone else it mutates to their own creative thing and they then become patient zero.

My son and I were having a conversation about building things and he stonewalled me with this question:

"Dad, what if there was no creativity in the world?"

"Uhhh, well..."

He continued, "I mean, do you think we could even survive."

"Nah I don't think so. If there were no people sharing what they loved to do and how they do it how could things ever get made or get better"

"Hehe, yeah it would be like we only had vanilla ice cream but humanity needed neo, neopolo...."

"Neapolitan ice cream?"

"Yeah, that's the one... You know dad, it would really be hard to live on earth and not be creative."

I have six beautiful children. Each one is unique. My wife and I have put all of them in front of technology, programming, hardware, art, literature and the like and something amazing has happened every time we've done that. They discover a little more about themselves each time they do.

My son **Caden** (11 years) loves to program, play music and read.

My son **Jonah** (9 years) loves hardware, soldering and builds on the IoT (Internet of Things).

My son **Levi** (7 years) loves to build things with Legos or any other materials he can find.

My son **Dylan** (5 years) loves to adventure in the wilderness, find materials and build weapons and tools with them

My daughter **Ruthie** (3 years) loves to paint and solder with me

My daughter **AvaJoy** (2 years) loves to be a mad scientist and test out everything (especially her parents).

I've tried to be the same dad and they've had the same amazing mom - so why the difference in passions? Because over time, despite what we have taught and other people's impact in their lives, the things they read and experience has created a whole new creativity virus in them. Without humanity's legacy of creativity and others before us having the courage to share what they love with the world we'd be challenged with the additional burden of cutting new paths. As my son pointed out using a frozen sweetened flavored bovine secretion (ice cream) as an example, "it would really be hard to live on earth and not be creative."

Do you smile when you're building stuff or writing code (smiles on the inside count too)?

Do you want to share your latest hack with your kids, friends or spouse?

When was the last time your heart raced when you

were on the cusp of solving a really hard problem?

Ripples not wrinkles.

At the end of your life you'll look back and see the handful of decisions that have changed the course of your life and the lives of others around you. It's like throwing a stone in a pond. These are your "ripples" - the things you did that genuinely made an impact on something or someone. The hope is that you have more ripples than you do wrinkles.

Do you remember that choice I was eluding to earlier? We all get to make it every day. This is the same choice that people like Ada Lovelace[81], Rear Admiral Grace Hopper[82], Markus Persson[83], Jonathan Gillette a.k.a._- why the lucky stiff[84] and so many more before us have made.

We can either choose to be **exceptional** or we can choose to be **mediocre**. No matter what we choose the result will inevitably infect our family and friends. Being exceptional is not having ninja-like skills when you cut up vegetables or being right all the time. By no means does exceptional mean famous, rich or successful by the worlds standards; though sometimes

---

[81]https://en.wikipedia.org/wiki/Ada_Lovelace

[82]https://en.wikipedia.org/wiki/Grace_Hopper#UNIVAC

[83]https://en.wikipedia.org/wiki/Markus_Persson

[84]https://en.wikipedia.org/wiki/Why_the_lucky_stiff

those are the byproducts.

No, what I am referring to is a choice to find, share and do what you love to do without wavering. Being a nerd in the purest sense in the place where you cannot help but smile.

Find what you love to do, share it with others and you will have achieved **Nerd Life Balance**.

There is a philosophy in software development around sharing. It's called open source software (OSS). There's nothing magical about it other than the fact that this simple idea can be tremendously powerful. It is meant to be a collaborative effort, where people work on the source collectively as a community and share it openly with the world. Think of it in terms of the wisdom of the masses; where there is something to be done, and it can not only get done faster with a group of people, but it can get done "better." We live in a time where there is so little friction to sharing things that some people become over night, unintentional celebrities. Some of the shared content has very little use while other content forms the very foundations of the internet - like a good cat video montage.

I've noticed a recent shift in things that I think is a cultural renaissance. More and more kids are posting videos and content on hacking the internet of things. They are talking more about making games rather than playing them. They are actively becoming makers and creators and walking away from being just users.

We have a rare opportunity to make a difference and an impact that will change things for future generations of makers. We can choose to build things, experience life and the things we love alone or we can choose to open source our life. It's a choice followed up by an action.

I know it's hard to believe. You might be thinking: "Can it really be that simple?", or "Can we collectively come together and make an impact on our families, friends and this fantastically crazy landscape we call our home?" I think we can. I know we can. All we have to do is start sharing the things we love with those we love. Make a difference with the time you have. Make an impact and share your individual creativity with everyone! Make something and share it.

OPEN SOURCE YOUR LIFE

Project: Hello World

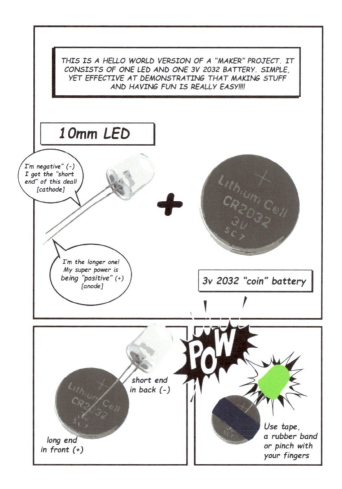

Materials

- 10m LED (really any size would work)
- CR2032 3V battery
- Fingers or tape

Project: Playing with matches

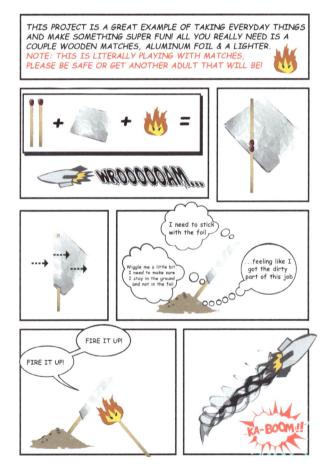

Materials

- 2 matches (strike anywhere matches generally work well)
- Aluminum foil (3in x 3in)
- Dirt (or some place to firmly plant the "rocket")

Project: Magnetic Appeal

Materials

- 1.5 oz cooking oil
- Magnetic ink (Most MICR toner refill kits will work)
- A small pan or bowl
- A magnet with approximately 25-100lb lift

Contributors

Nick Floyd[85]
Rebecca Floyd
Scott Hanselman[86]

---

[85]http://archcoder.com/
[86]http://hanselman.com

www.ingramcontent.com/pod-product-compliance
Lightning Source LLC
Chambersburg PA
CBHW041151050326
40690CB00001B/433